IT'S HARD TO BE HIP OVER
THIRTY . . . AND OTHER
TRAGEDIES OF MARRIED LIFE
and
PEOPLE & OTHER AGGRAVATIONS

Persephone Book N° 12
Published by Persephone Books Ltd 1999
Reprinted 2004

First published in the United States in 1968 and 1971, and in the
UK in 1973 by Angus & Robertson as It's Hard To Be Hip
over Thirty, *and* People & Other Aggravations

Endpapers taken from a 1968 Liberty's fabric called 'Bangles',
thought to have been exported to the United States in that year.
© Liberty of London Prints Ltd

Typeset in ITC Baskerville by Keystroke,
Jacaranda Lodge, Wolverhampton

Colour by Banbury Litho

Printed and bound by Biddles, King's Lynn

ISBN 1 903155 01 0

Persephone Books Ltd
59 Lamb's Conduit Street
London WC1N 3NB
020 7242 9292

www.persephonebooks.co.uk

IT'S HARD TO BE HIP OVER

THIRTY . . . AND OTHER

TRAGEDIES OF MARRIED LIFE

and

PEOPLE & OTHER AGGRAVATIONS

by

JUDITH VIORST

with a new preface by

THE AUTHOR

PERSEPHONE BOOKS
LONDON

CONTENTS

PEOPLE & OTHER AGGRAVATIONS

PREFACE

In early 1960, when I married, I planned to be a terrific wife
and mother within the context of a creative family life that in
no way at all resembled the conventional middle-class one I
had left behind in the suburbs of New Jersey. I promised
myself to wear a filmy peignoir and a touch of perfume at
breakfast, where my husband and I would argue over Plato's
philosopher-kings while a Bach cantata played softly in the
background. We would, so went my fantasy, be the married-
with-children version of that cutest of cute couples – de
Beauvoir and Sartre – our sexual and intellectual fervour
undiminished by the imperatives of domesticity.

By 1967 I was the mother of three young sons, and assailed
by domesticity's imperatives. My morning scenario was a
distant dream. I wore a faded corduroy robe with spit-up on
the shoulder – no perfume – at breakfast, where my husband
and I would argue over how often to phone his parents while
the children squabbled noisily in the background. No one
could possibly ever mistake me for Jean-Paul Sartre's Simone,
or even for my younger pre-marital self. My husband and I
were looking awfully conventional middle-class. What in the
world had become of us, of me?

At first this collision between my expectations and my
reality made me cry. Then, slowly, it made me shake my head
in bemusement. And then it made me sit down and start

writing the poems which became the book *It's Hard to Be Hip Over Thirty and Other Tragedies of Married Life.*

I had been writing poems since the age of seven, but until the 1960s my writings were dark, despairing, and littered with corpses. My very first effort, in fact, was an anguished ode to my dead parents, both of whom were alive and well and quite unnerved by my killing them off in verse. My subsequent writings offered dead dogs, dead soldiers, dead lovers, one entire dead family, and, in my teen-age years, 'Death and desire crumpled in a corner/And I in black, the solitary mourner.' I finally figured out that this high mortality rate derived from my mother's fondness for Poe's bleak 'Annabel Lee,' which featured a fair maiden who died young and wound up in a sepulchre down by the sea. Having heard my mother reciting 'Annabel' on numerous occasions, I believe I became convinced that a poem couldn't *be* a poem unless it had a dead body in it.

Though not an especially morbid girl, I felt quite at home with sepulchres down by the sea.

By the time I began writing *It's Hard to Be Hip*, however, I was in a different place: a place where I had a carpool, weekly duties at the co-op nursery school, a playpen in my living room, and Gerber's strained bananas in my hair. A place where my most urgent questions were answered not by Plato but by Dr. Spock. A place where the many challenges of marriage and the family sometimes made me feel as if my only two choices were homicide – or humour.

I chose humour.

And so I wrote of the shocks that start to kick in as soon as

The honeymoon is over
And we find that dining by candlelight makes us squint.

And I looked at the many dumb quarrels that erupt when we fail to avoid discussions like

Suppose I died, which one of our friends would he marry?

And I contrasted last year, when we

Threw clever little cocktail parties in our discerningly
*   eclectic living room*
With the Spanish rug and the hand-carved Chinese chest
*   and the lucite chairs*

with this year, when

. . . we have a nice baby
And Spock on the second shelf of our Chinese chest.

I also faced up to the inroads of materialism, conceding that

Spiritual is hard without the cash
To pay the plumber to unstop the sink
And pay a lady to come clean and iron
So every other Friday I can think about
Great literature and philosophy.

As for sex, I admitted that, what with flannel nightgowns and socks for freezing feet, it wasn't all that sexy anymore.

And yet, in spite of the unsentimental eye I cast upon the married state, I poetically concluded that married is better.

I also concluded that, although marriage has many features that dampen the fires of passion, we can still find in it something called true love.

When these poems were published a great many people who weren't even my relatives and friends bought my book and wrote to say they liked it. In their letters they told me, in vast detail, about their personal lives which, they insisted, were very much like mine.

'I am a short, plump, blonde Protestant woman who lives on a farm in the Middle West,' said my favourite letter, 'and you are a tall, thin, dark Jewish woman who lives in a city on the East Coast – and we lead the same life.'

I loved that letter. I loved making that kind of connection, loved finding the points of contact buried beneath the apparent differences, loved discovering that we were all in the same matrimonial boat – dealing with the disappointments, savouring the delights, and doing what we could to stay afloat.

I also loved the fact that after trying, so long, to get my poems into print, I had become a professional published poet who was actually earning money writing poems. And this meant that, in addition to the boost my success provided my budget and ego, my publishers wished me to write another book.

By this time, though I continued to have plenty to say about the married state, my attention and pen had also been captured by the astounding transformations of the Sixties. The new music, the new fashions, the new sexual freedom, the peace movement and civil rights movement and women's

movement had altered the world I had grown up in almost beyond recognition. I had touched on some of these changes in *It's Hard to Be Hip*, and they had certainly made an impact on my life where, in addition to the accoutrements of domesticity, I had acquired a beaded headband, a mini-dress composed of green and orange and shocking-pink plastic squares, a pair of white Go Go boots, and a feathered necklace which, my husband insisted, looked very much as if a pigeon had crashed into my chest and expired. I belonged to peace organizations and attended fund-raisers for civil-rights organizations and spent weekends picketing the White House or marching on the Pentagon or assembling at the Washington Monument with my little boys and a cast of thousands, all of us shouting, 'What do we want? Freedom! When do we want it? Now!' when we weren't shouting, 'What do we want? Peace? When do we want it? Now!' I learned to distinguish Pop art from Op art, the Twist from the Frug, and Ringo from George from Paul from John. I once went to jail for five hours for an act of anti-war civil disobedience. I even, on a few occasions, inhaled.

But in any contest between the political and psychedelic seductions of the Sixties and taking my kids to buy sneakers, the sneakers invariably won. And though I watched in fascination as people not that much younger than I turned on, tuned in, dropped out, made love not war, and gave up medical school to become harpsichord tuners, I remained entrenched in my married-with-children mode. I was too plain to be one of the Beautiful People and too straight to be a hippie, but I wanted to write about them. And so, in *People &*

Other Aggravations, I observed – from my sticky seat in the family station wagon – the brave new world I uneasily was living in.

I offered, for instance, my highly ambivalent views of the Women's Liberation Movement, acknowledging that

> *When it's snowing and I put on all the galoshes*
> *While he reads the paper,*
> *Then I want to become a*
> *Women's Liberation Movement woman.*
> *And when it's snowing and he looks for the taxi*
> *While I wait in the lobby,*
> *Then I don't.*

Noting that 'I like to keep up with the new aberrations', I examined the purported benefits of spouse-swapping, about which

> *It's claimed that the switching of partners produces*
> *A soundness of body and mind*
> *And feelings of intimate group satisfaction*
> *That couples can't manage to find*
> *In cook-outs and bridge clubs and zoning board meetings*
> *And fund drives to build the school gym . . .*

I also wrote a poem about my cousin Alan the drop-out, who

> *With brains like an Einstein or Goldberg*
> *And a guaranteed future in Orlon,*
> *Is living in worse than a cellar*
> *With a girlfriend a mother could die from,*

According to mine.

And in the days before the phrase 'politically correct' had made its appearance, I wrote about Sally and Stu, who strived to be 'politically perfect'

> *By displaying aggressive bumper stickers,*
> *Boycotting non-returnable bottles . . . ,*
> *Picketing profusely,*
> *And including, at every Christmas party,*
> *One unwed mother, one well-intentioned bomber, and the*
>   *maid.*

People included, along with the spouse-swappers, Alan the drop-out, and the politically perfect Sally and Stu, more conventional types: like Ida, the one who suffers. Like the flirty lady next door. And like David, who is dying to get married but keeps finding compelling reasons not to. There is also 'I', a woman who worries about her laugh lines, starts a new diet every Monday, wishes she 'were one of those spunky women who dash off to Africa with a cleverly packed over-night bag and a pith helmet,' and still secretly believes that if Paul Newman really got to know her he'd divorce his wife.

That 'I' of *People & Other Aggravations*, like the 'I' of *It's Hard to Be Hip*, both is and isn't me. I write poems, not autobiography, and I like to say that when it comes to using my private life in verse, I tell the truth, but not the whole truth, and certainly not nothing but the truth. The 'I' of my books includes me and all of my friends, and also strangers, whose lives I've heard about or read about or asked about or

eavesdropped on. It's meant to be the 'I' of an over-thirty wife and mother Everywoman.

I hadn't originally planned to follow this 'I' through subsequent decades, but that's what I've done, documenting the forties and fifties and just this minute completing *Suddenly Sixty and Other Shocks of Later Life*. Each of my books is very much set in the time in which it was written, and some of the images in *Hip* and *People* are so very 1960s that they only work as pure nostalgia. I do believe, however, that most of the poems in *Hip* and *People* remain relevant no matter what calendar year they're being read in. The collision between our marital expectations and married reality will always be a major shock to our system, our children will always dribble on our lives, we will – no matter what kind of skin cream we buy – acquire laugh lines, and we will constantly struggle to figure out who *we* are vis à vis the people around us.

With luck we'll also figure out that laughing at ourselves can really help.

I need to say, however, that a sense of humour about one's imperfect existence takes time to ripen. I wouldn't want anyone thinking that I have been chuckling merrily merrily through the years. But although I have a world-class gift for complaining, complaints don't do much for oneself or anyone else. So after crying, whining, moaning 'Why me!' and, whenever possible, blaming my husband, I have managed to find some humour in the 'tragedies' and 'aggravations' of life.

Judith Viorst
Washington D.C.
1999

IT'S HARD TO BE HIP OVER

THIRTY . . . AND OTHER

TRAGEDIES OF MARRIED LIFE

and

PEOPLE & OTHER AGGRAVATIONS

TO MILTON

IT'S HARD TO BE HIP OVER
THIRTY . . . AND OTHER
TRAGEDIES OF MARRIED LIFE

MARRIAGE AND THE FAMILIES

My mother was grateful
He wasn't barefoot.
His mother was grateful
I wasn't pregnant.

My father was grateful
He wasn't of a different race, color, or creed.
His father was grateful
I wasn't tubercular or divorced.

My sister was grateful
Her husband was richer and taller.
His sister was grateful
She had a master's degree and a better nose.

My cousin in luggage was grateful
He didn't expect a discount.
His cousin the dentist was grateful
I didn't need root canal.

My aunts and my uncles were grateful
He came from a nice family in New Jersey even though he
    wore sunglasses in the living room which is usually a sign
    of depravity.

His aunts and his uncles were grateful
I came from a nice family in New Jersey even though I lived
    in Greenwich Village which is usually a sign of depravity
    also.

I should be pleased.

But when I think of the catered wedding in Upper Montclair,
With the roast sirloin of beef dinner,
The souvenir photo album,
And the matches with our names in raised gold letters,
And when I think of the Ronson lighters, the savings bonds,
    the cut glass, and the sugars and creamers both sterling
    and silver plate,
Then I wish
That they weren't
So grateful.

THE HONEYMOON IS OVER

The honeymoon is over
And he has left for work
Whistling something obvious from La Bohème
And carrying a brown calfskin attaché case
I never dreamed he was capable of owning,
Having started the day
With ten pushups and a cold shower
Followed by a hearty breakfast.

(What do we actually have in common?)

The honeymoon is over
And I am dry-mopping the floor
In a green Dacron dry-mopping outfit from Saks,
Wondering why I'm not dancing in the dark,
Or rejecting princes,
Or hearing people gasp at my one-man show,
My god, so beautiful and so gifted!

(The trouble is I never knew a prince.)

The honeymoon is over
And we find that dining by candlelight makes us squint,
And that all the time

I was letting him borrow my comb and hang up his wet
   raincoat in my closet,
I was really waiting
To stop letting him.
And that all the time
He was saying how he loved my chicken pot pie,
He was really waiting
To stop eating it.

(I guess they call this getting to know each other.)

A GOOD CATCH

Although he is still wearing his college ring,
And driving a white Imperial,
And taking girls to supper clubs where the entire meal is
    served flambé
Because he still thinks the more flames the better,
Freddie the bachelor
Is what is known in New Jersey as
A good catch.

He has waves in his hair,
Caps on his teeth,
A manicure on his nails,
And what is known in New Jersey as
A nice physique. Also
A clean bill of health,
A great sense of humor,
And a steady job,
With what is known in New Jersey as
Room for advancement. Also
Serious interests
Such as reading and Broadway plays
That are not even musicals.

Although he still remembers the fraternity handshake,
And the football cheers,
And is still singing in girls' ears while dancing
Because someone once told him that singing in ears is sexy,
Freddie the bachelor
Is what is known in New Jersey as
A good catch.

He has cashmere sweaters,
A Danish-modern apartment,
A retirement plan,
And what is known in New Jersey as
Sound investments. Also
A way with children,
Consideration for others,
And what is known in New Jersey as
A good head on his shoulders. Also
Important contacts
Such as a nephew of the Congressman
From Flushing.

And whenever my husband is showing
What is known in New Jersey as no respect
For my mother,
She tells about Freddie the bachelor,
Who never talks back and is such
A good catch.

MAYBE WE'LL MAKE IT

If I quit hoping he'll show up with flowers, and
He quits hoping I'll squeeze him an orange, and
I quit shaving my legs with his razor, and
He quits wiping his feet with my face towel, and
We avoid discussions like
Is he really smarter than I am, or simply more glib,
Maybe we'll make it.

If I quit looking to prove that he's hostile, and
He quits looking for dust on the tables, and
I quit inviting Louise with the giggle, and
He quits inviting Jerome with the complex, and
We avoid discussions like
Suppose I died, which one of our friends would he marry,
Maybe we'll make it.

We've fully examined James Reston, the war,
John Updike, religion, the Renaissance, CORE,
And on all major issues we're for and against
The same things.
Yet somehow we've managed to not miss a fight.
He tells me there's nothing to nosh on at night.
I tell him that no one can sleep with a light in her eyes,

Not to mention
He takes too much time in the bathroom. But

If I quit clearing the plates while he's eating, and
He quits clearing his throat while I'm speaking, and
I quit implying I could have done better, and
He quits implying he wishes I had, and
We avoid discussions like
Does his mother really love him, or is she simply one of
    those over-possessive, devouring women who can't let go,
Maybe we'll make it.

NICE BABY

Last year I talked about black humor and the impact of the
    common market on the European economy and
Threw clever little cocktail parties in our discerningly
    eclectic living room
With the Spanish rug and the hand-carved Chinese chest
    and the lucite chairs and
Was occasionally hungered after by highly placed men in
    communications, but
This year we have a nice baby
And pablum drying on our Spanish rug,
And I talk about nursing versus sterilization
While the men in communications
Hunger elsewhere.

Last year I studied flamenco and had my ears pierced and
Served an authentic fondue on the Belgian marble table of
    our discerningly eclectic dining area, but
This year we have a nice baby
And Spock on the second shelf of our Chinese chest,
And instead of finding myself I am doing my best
To find a sitter
For the nice baby banging the Belgian marble with his cup
While I heat the oven up
For the TV dinners.

Last year I had a shampoo and set every week and
Slept an unbroken sleep beneath the Venetian chandelier of
  our discerningly eclectic bedroom, but
This year we have a nice baby,
And Gerber's strained bananas in my hair,
And gleaming beneath the Venetian chandelier,
A diaper pail, a portacrib, and him,
A nice baby, drooling on our antique satin spread
While I smile and say how nice. It is often said
That motherhood is very maturing.

THE SUBURBANITES

They love it here.
They say
New York is a dirty town. Full of
  sex fiends,
  and dope fiends,
  and irresponsible people crossing against the light,
  ruthless people writing television commercials for money,
  hostile people riding the IRT.
  (You could sit forever in Chock Full O'Nuts,
  they say,
  and never meet a person you could trust.)
And New York is full of
  pop artists,
  op artists,
  and avant-garde people who know which Westerns to like,
  sneaky people hiding behind dark glasses,
  heartless people ignoring screams of help.
  (You could drop dead in the middle of Times Square,
  they say,
  and no one would even offer a glass of water.)
And New York is full of
  litterbugs,
  the Mafia,
  aggressive women going to work in hats,

nervous people with psychiatrists on Central Park West,
wicked people living with other wicked people to whom
    they are not married,
emancipated people thinking it's smart to talk back to
    their mothers,
greedy slumlords,
sinister foreigners,
and uppity neighbors.
(You could live your whole life on East Sixty-fifth,
they say,
and the Welcome Wagon would never bring a cake.)

CHOICES

We've met the fun couples
Who own works of art
That are strawberry malteds in plaster,
And watch television
Only to see the commercials,
And use words like life style and panache.

And we've met the boycott-the-supermarket people
Who oppose certain conservative instant puddings
And support certain progressive canned vegetables
In addition to voter registration, busing, and immediate
    withdrawal.

And we've met the above-reproach crowd
Who are signed up for
Cancer,
Heart disease,
Stroke,
A booth at the annual book fair,
And he goes to sewer meetings in tweed jackets
With leather elbow patches
While she exchanges recipes
At brunches.

And we've met the social leaders
Who know how to act at horse shows,
And their ancestors always come from the British Isles.

And we've met the self-improvers
Who buy quality paperbacks,
Season tickets to theaters in the round,
And Brentano reproductions.

And we can't decide
Who we want them to think
We are.

STRIKING BACK

When a husband tells a wife
Stop screaming at the children
And he isn't crazy about the drapes
And why doesn't she learn where Thailand is
And maybe she should cut her hair
(All of which, needless to say, are implicit attacks on her
Intelligence,
Taste,
Desirability,
And maternal instincts)
A wife
Can only
Strike back.

So sometimes I try
My mother's technique
Which is silence for a week,
A brooding stare into the ruined future,
And no rouge for that look of
You are making me so miserable you are giving me
A fatal illness.

It occasionally works.

And sometimes I try
Weeping, cursing, expressions of bitter remorse,
And don't ever expect to see the children again,
Which I often follow with phone calls pricing suites
At expensive hotels.

I've had limited success.

There is also
The psychoanalytic confrontation
Which entails informing him
(More, of course, in sorrow than in anger)
That his sadistic treatment of those who love him is a sign of
    unconscious feelings of inadequacy and
He needs help.

I've dropped this approach.

But there is always
Total recall
During which all the wrongs he has done me since first we
    met
Are laid before him.
And when this is combined
With refusing to go to the Greenberg's annual costume party,
Tossing and moaning in my sleep,
And threatening to commit suicide, take a lover, and drop
    out of the PTA because why try to save the school system
    when my entire universe is falling apart,

I start to feel
I'm really
Striking back.

THE OTHER WOMAN

The other woman
Never smells of Ajax or Spaghetti-O,
And was bored with Bob Dylan
A year before we had heard of him,
And is a good sport about things like flat tires and no hot
    water,
Because it's easier to be a good sport
When you're not married.

The other woman
Never has tired blood,
And can name the best hotels in Acapulco
As readily as we can name detergents,
And wears a chiffon peignoir instead of a corduroy bathrobe,
Because it's easier to try harder
When you're not married.

The other woman
Never has to look at Secret Squirrel,
And spends her money on fun furs
While we are spending ours on obstetricians,
And can make a husband feel that he is wanted,
Because it's easier to want a husband
When you're not married.

IT'S HARD TO BE HIP OVER THIRTY

All around New York
Perfect girls with hairpieces and fishnet jumpsuits
Sit in their art nouveau apartments
Discussing things like King Kong
With people like Rudolph Nureyev.

Meanwhile, the rest of us,
Serving Crispy Critters to grouchy three-year-olds
And drinking our Metrecal,
Dream of snapping our fingers to the music
If only we knew when to snap.

But it's hard to be hip over thirty
When everyone else is nineteen,
When the last dance we learned was the Lindy
And the last we heard, girls who looked like Barbra Streisand
Were trying to do something about it.

We long to be kicky and camp – but
The maid only comes once a week.
And since we have to show up for the car pool,
Orgiastic pot parties with cool Negroes who say 'funky' and
      'man'
Seem rather impractical.

The Love Song of J. Alfred Prufrock,
Which we learned line by line long ago,
Doesn't swing, we are told, on East Tenth Street,
Where all the perfect girls are switched-on or tuned-in or
    miscegenated,
But never over thirty
Trying hard
To be hip.

A VISIT FROM MY MOTHER-IN-LAW

My mother-in-law
Comes to visit
With her own apron,
Her own jar of Nescafé,
And the latest news.

Uncle Leo,
She's sorry to say,
Is divorcing Aunt Pearl,
Whose sister Bernice
Is having
A nervous breakdown.
The week
That they spent in Miami
It rained every day,
And her health,
Though she isn't complaining,
Has never been worse.
The lady upstairs
With the limp
Was attacked in broad daylight,
And Seymour her nephew
Has cataracts, flu,
And no job.

My husband,
She thinks she should mention,
Looks thin as a rail,
And the children,
It hurts her to hear,
Are coughing again.
Belle's son,
Only forty years old,
Dropped dead Friday morning,
And don't even bother
To ask
About Cousin Rose.

I don't think I will.

MONEY

Once I aspired to
Humble black turtleneck sweaters
And spare unheated rooms
With the Kama Sutra, a few madrigals, and
Great literature and philosophy.

Once I considered money
Something to be against
On the grounds that
Credit cards,
Installment-plan buying,
And a joint checking account
Could never coexist with
Great literature and philosophy.

Once I believed
That the only kind of marriage I could respect
Was a spiritual relationship
Between two wonderfully spiritual human beings
Who would never argue about money
Because they would be too busy arguing about
Great literature and philosophy.

I changed my mind,

Having discovered that

Spiritual is hard without the cash
To pay the plumber to unstop the sink
And pay a lady to come clean and iron
So every other Friday I can think about
Great literature and philosophy.

No one ever offers us a choice
Between the Kama Sutra and a yacht.
We're always selling out for diaper service
And other drab necessities that got ignored in
Great literature and philosophy.

A jug of wine, a loaf of bread, and thou
No longer will suffice. I must confess
My consciousness is frequently expanded
By Diners' Club, American Express, and things undreamed
    of in
Great literature and philosophy.

I saw us walking hand-in-hand through life,
But now it's clear we really need two cars.
I looked with such contempt at power mowers,
And now, alas, that power mower's ours.
It seems I'm always reaching for my charge plates,
When all I'd planned to reach for were the stars,
Great literature and philosophy.

THE FIX-UP

I have this friend Muriel who is attractive and intelligent and
    terribly understanding and loyal and
My husband has this friend Ralph who is handsome and
    witty and essentially very sincere and
Since they weren't engaged or even tacitly committed
The least we could do, I said, is fix them up,
So I cooked this very nice boned chicken breasts with lemon-
    cream sauce and
Put on a little Herb Alpert in the background and
Before Muriel came I told Ralph how she was attractive and
    intelligent and terribly understanding and loyal and
After Muriel came I drew out Ralph to show how he was witty
    and very sincere and
When dinner was over my husband and I did the dishes
Leaving Ralph and Muriel to get acquainted
With a little Petula Clark in the background and
We listened while they discovered that they both loved Mel
    Brooks and hated Los Angeles and agreed that the
    Supremes had lost their touch and
He insisted on taking her home even though she lived in the
    opposite direction and
The next day he phoned to ask is that what I call attractive,
    after which
She phoned to ask is that what I call sincere

And from now on
I cook lemon-cream sauce
For young marrieds.

WHERE IS IT WRITTEN?

Where is it written
That husbands get twenty-five-dollar lunches and invitations
    to South America for think conferences while
Wives get Campbell's black bean soup and a trip to the
    firehouse with the first grade and
Where is it written
That husbands get to meet beautiful lady lawyers and
    beautiful lady professors of Ancient History and beautiful
    sculptresses and heiresses and poetesses while
Wives get to meet the checker with the acne at the Safeway
    and
Where is it written
That husbands get a nap and the Super Bowl on Sundays
    while
Wives get to help color in the coloring book and
Where is it written
That husbands get ego gratification, emotional support, and
    hot tea in bed for ten days when they have the sniffles
    while
Wives get to give it to them?

And if a wife should finally decide
Let *him* take the shoes to the shoemaker and the children to
    the pediatrician and the dog to the vet while she takes up

something like brain surgery or transcendental
    meditation,
Where is it written
That she always has to feel
Guilty?

THE COCKTAIL PARTY

The hostess is passing the sour-cream dip and the carrots,
    and
The husband is mixing up something with rum in the
    blender, and
The mothers are finishing teething and starting on ear
    aches, and
The ones with the tan are describing their trip to St. Thomas,
    and
The fellow they swore was funnier than Joey Bishop
Is discussing tax breaks
With the fellow they swore was funnier than Mort Sahl,
and
The hostess is passing the eggs with the mayonnaise-curry,
    and
The husband is being risqué with a blonde in the foyer, and
The mothers are finishing ear aches and starting on day
    camps, and
The one who can play the piano is playing Deep Purple, and
The fellow they swore was smarter than David Susskind
Is discussing field goals
With the fellow they swore was smarter than Max Lerner,
and
The hostess is passing the heat-and-serve pigs in a blanket,
    and

The husband is passing out cold on the coats in the
    bedroom, and
The mothers are finishing day camps and starting on sex
    play, and
The one on the diet is saying she's not even hungry, and
The fellow they swore was cuter than Warren Beatty
Is discussing drain pipes
With the fellow they swore was cuter than Michael Caine,
and
I'm not as out of place
As I wish I were.

GETTING READY

Every summer
I go to places like Truro
With the three children, my husband, and a mother's helper
Who is always a lithe, bronze, sexually emancipated
    nineteen-year-old
Who is always playing tennis with my husband
While I sweep out the sand,
Remove bathing suits from the garbage disposal,
And entertain large numbers of strangers
With marinated artichokes and gin.

But this summer
I have given the kids
To an overweight, sexually inhibited, sixty-year-old mother's
    helper –
My mother.
And, having persuaded myself
That miniskirts and varicose veins are not, in all cases,
Mutually exclusive,
I have purchased a complete love-in drop-out wardrobe
From the suburban branch of Franklin Simon.

I have, in addition,
Acquired the conditional perfect tense from Berlitz,

Stomach muscles from yoga,
Long hair from a second cousin who gets it wholesale,
And, from impeccable sources on the New Left,
The latest views on riots, heart transplants, our suicidal
   foreign policy, and Jewish novelists.

I am, I feel, ready at last for France.
I only hope that France is ready for me.

ABOARD THE SS FRANCE

I was expecting
Gay flirtations on the promenade deck,
Smoldering glances across the mid-morning bouillon,
An improper proposal or two
Deftly turned away with regretful sighs.
But no one asked.

So I sit in the smoking room of the SS France
Showing pictures of the kids
To a White Plains widow with heartburn
While some very clean teachers on grants
Discuss the cost of living
With a dry-goods merchant from Nice
And several men who look like my Uncle Max
Are forgetting the bad backs and the high blood pressure
Long enough to do the bossa nova
With clerk-typists in Macy's pants suits.

And though I have tried
The heated swimming pool,
The movies, the music, the champagne,
The foie gras de Siorac à la gelée au Xérès,
Not to mention one gala,
One spectacular,

And plenty of ping-pong,
I keep finding
Exchange students singing Old MacDonald,
Ladies in imitation Puccis comparing laxatives,
And countless adolescents named Stevie and Marv.

So the next time I want a fleeting moment of passion
With the wind and the salt spray in my hair
And someone bitter but basically worthwhile
Laying his soul bare
Beside me, at the rail,
I think I'll take the Hudson River Day Line.

IN DEAUVILLE

In Deauville
Everyone but us
Is a fading French actress,
An Italian polo player,
An obscene American novelist,
Or a pretender to some throne,
All of whom are exchanging quips and barbs
And other chic things
With heiresses, scions, magnates,
Doomed but gallant contessas,
And dégagé Parisians in maroon ascots and four-inch
    sideburns.

In Deauville
Everyone but us
Is playing chemin de fer
The way my mother plays in the Tuesday gin club,
And buying horses
The way my father buys a good cigar,
And telling the waiter the champagne smells of cork
With the assurance of those
Who have never saved trading stamps
Or attended a swim club cook-out.

And even if we had arrived
With an Alfa Romeo,
A yacht,
His and her dinner clothes by Pierre Cardin,
And a handwritten introduction from Francoise Sagan,
They would still know
We did not belong
In Deauville.

IN PARIS

I am (where else?) at the Deux Magots
Moodily drinking a pernod
And trying to think thoughts
Jean-Paul Sartre would respect
And trying to convey the impression
That I am someone with a rich full inner life
Instead of someone
Who gets palpitations
When the washer-dryer breaks down.

We've chosen a très charmant hotel
With a w.c. in the hall and an elevator
That was designed by Marat or de Sade.
And when I gaze at Notre Dame and the Arch of Triumph,
Having cultural insights about Gothic architecture and the
    vanity of power and similar transcendent topics,
You could think I was someone who subscribes to The
    Kenyon Review,
Instead of someone
Who reads
Can This Marriage Be Saved?

Meanwhile, the Georges V ladies
Are getting the facials and comb-outs every morning,

After which they put on their little Chanels
And visit Hermès, the Dior boutique, and other crass,
    insensitive places.
And all those people with Kodaks
Are snapping more people with Kodaks
At the Eiffel Tower and other readily recognizable places.
And a thousand flower children
Are walking their beards and bells
Barefoot down the Boulevard Saint-Michel
And other psychedelic places.
And whom can I identify with now?

So I'm here (why not?) at the Deux Magots
Buying Le Monde in French although
I feel more secure with the Herald Tribune in English.
And in my heart of hearts I know
I should have come here years ago
When I had a total grasp of The Stranger and Gérard
    Philippe and the difference between a Cézanne and a
    Matisse without even peeking at the signatures,
And when I had never heard of Whip 'n Chill or contour
    diapers or term insurance,
And when I would have been someone with unplumbed
    hidden depths,
Instead of someone
With color television
In the rumpus room.

BACK HOME

The French do not understand
Ronald Reagan for President,
Or peanut butter and jelly sandwiches for lunch.
And I do not understand
The franc,
The Renault R-10,
Or the liver.

The French do not understand
The Peck & Peck girl,
Or paper bags.
And I do not understand
Their telephones,
Their Général,
Or their Gauloises bleues.

But today
When I was defrosting the refrigerator,
And telling the laundry no starch,
And asking the butcher to cut off all the fat,
And wiping fingerpaints from the floor of the co-op nursery,
And catching up on
Poverty,
Escalation,

Crime in the streets,
The crisis in the schools,
H. Rap Brown,
Mary Worth,
And the Beautiful People,
I find
I do not understand
America.

SEX IS NOT SO SEXY ANYMORE

I bring the children one more glass of water.
I rub the hormone night cream on my face.
Then after I complete the isometrics,
I greet my husband with a warm embrace,

A vision in my long-sleeved flannel nightgown
And socks (because my feet are always freezing),
Gulping tranquilizers for my nerve ends,
And Triaminic tablets for my wheezing.

Our blue electric blanket's set for toasty.
Our red alarm clock's set at seven-thirty.
I tell him that we owe the grocer plenty.
He tells me that his two best suits are dirty.

Last year I bought him Centaur for his birthday.
(They promised he'd become half-man, half-beast.)
Last year he bought me something black and lacy.
(They promised I'd go mad with lust, at least.)

Instead my rollers clink upon the pillow
And his big toenail scrapes against my skin.
He rises to apply a little Chap Stick.
I ask him to bring back two Bufferin.

Oh somewhere there are lovely little boudoirs
With Porthault sheets and canopies and whips.
He lion-hunts in Africa on weekends.
She measures thirty-three around the hips.

Their eyes engage across the brandy snifters.
He runs his fingers through her Kenneth hair.
The kids are in the other wing with nanny.
The sound of violins is everywhere.

In our house there's the sound of dripping water.
It's raining and he never patched the leak.
He grabs the mop and I get out the bucket.
We both agree to try again next week.

THE DIVORCE

Mark and June
Who were such a perfect match
That everyone used to say how perfect they were
Are getting a divorce, because
He only likes spy movies and Audrey Hepburn movies and
  movies that leave you feeling good and
She only likes early Chaplin movies and movies with
  subtitles and movies that leave you feeling rotten and
He thinks Maria Montessori is a fascist and
She thinks Will and Ariel Durant have an unwholesome
  relationship and
He says she should pick up his socks and drop them in the
  hamper and
She says he should.

Mark is keeping the Honda
And June is keeping the Mercedes and the Picasso
  lithographs
As well as the Early American hutch table that they bought
  for a song in Philadelphia, because
He says it wouldn't have killed her to go on a camping trip
  sometimes and
She says it wouldn't have killed him to put on the velvet
  smoking jacket she gave him for Christmas sometimes

and
He thinks Marshall McLuhan is a fascist and
She thinks Richard and Pat Nixon have an unwholesome
    relationship and
He only likes paintings when you know what it's a painting of
    and
She only likes paintings when you don't.

June gets custody of the children
And Mark gets their dog, their orthodontia bills,
And visitation rights on alternate weekends, because
He thinks a great meal is shrimp cocktail and filet mignon
    and
She thinks a great meal is something like brains cooked in
    wine and
He says she is a fascist and
She says he and his mother have an unwholesome
    relationship and
He only likes women who'd rather make love than read
    Proust and
She only likes men who'd vice versa.

How come we thought they were such a perfect match?

INFIDELITY

In my burnt-orange Dynel lounging pajamas
With the rhinestone buttons,
I was, I concede, looking more abandoned than usual,
Which is probably the reason
Why my husband's best friend
Made overtures.

My pulse quickened,
And I could imagine . . .
   Cryptic conversations.
   Clandestine martinis.
   Tumultuous embraces.
   And me explaining
   That I can't slip away on Thursdays because of cub scouts.
   And that long kisses clog my sinuses.

Under the bridge table
His hand-sewn moccasins
Rubbed insistently against my Bernardo sandals,
While Dionne Warwick
Sang something suggestive
In stereo.

My lips trembled,

And I could imagine . . .
    Stolen weekends at a windswept beach.
    Waves pounding on the shore.
    And pounding on the door
    Of our motel hideaway,
    The Vice Squad.

Over the salt-free peanuts and diet soda
His contact lenses
Sought mine,
As I sucked in my stomach
And asked him,
Coffee or Sanka.

My throat tightened.
My lips trembled.
My pulse quickened . . .
    But aggravation
    Was all
    I could imagine.

MARRIED IS BETTER

There are those of us who gave up a promising career
As assistant to the editorial assistant to the editor
Or secretary to the private secretary of the executive producer,
And a glittering social life
Of boîtes, soirées, and happenings,
And romance in the form of
Brief encounters, moonlight and love songs, I can't live
    without you,
And so forth,
Because, as someone once put it,
Married is better.

Married is better
Than sitting on a blanket in Nantucket
Where you get blotches and a red nose instead of adorable
    freckles and golden brown,
Hoping that someone with whom you would not be caught
    dead
From September to June
Will invite you to dinner,
And it is better
Than riding a double chair lift up at Stowe
On your way to an expert trail and you're a beginner,
Hoping the fellow for whom you are risking your life
Will invite you to dinner.

And one night, when you land at Kennedy, and no one is
    there to meet you except your parents
And you suddenly realize that you never saw the Parthenon
    because you were too busy looking around for a Greek god,
You also suddenly realize
Married is better.

And married is better
Than an affair with a marvelous man
Who would leave his wife immediately except that she would
    slash her wrists and the children would cry.
So instead you drink his Scotch in your living room and
    never meet his friends because they might become
    disillusioned or tell,
And when it's your birthday it's his evening with the in-laws,
And when it's his birthday he can't even bring home your
    present
(Because of the slashed wrists and the crying and all),
And even though you have his body and soul while his wife
    only has his laundry and the same name,
You somehow begin to suspect
Married is better.

And married is better
Than the subway plus a crosstown bus every morning,
And tuna on toasted cheese bread, no lettuce, at Schrafft's,
And a bachelor-girl apartment with burlap and foam rubber
    and a few droll touches like a Samurai sword in the
    bathroom,
And going to the movies alone,

And worrying that one morning you'll wake up and discover
  you're an older woman,
And always projecting wholesome sexuality combined with
  independence, femininity, and tons of outside interests,
And never for a minute letting on
That deep in your heart you believe
Married is better.

THE GENERATION GAP

Our sons are growing up
And any day now
They'll be sniffing glue,
Smoking pot,
Slipping LSD into their cream of wheat,
And never trusting anyone over thirty,
Even parents
Who once sang Foggy Foggy Dew
In youth hostels,
And Freiheit
In trench coats on the Fire Island ferry.

Our sons are growing up
And any day now
They'll be burning draft cards,
Doubting the Warren Commission,
Saying God is dead,
And never trusting anyone over thirty,
Even parents
Who once deplored prejudice
In petitions,
And capital punishment
In unpublished letters to the Times.

Our sons are growing up
And any day now
They'll be doing their own thing,
Telling it like it is,
Denouncing the military-industrial complex,
And never trusting anyone over thirty,
Even parents
Who tried agitation
Before they did,
And alienation
Before they did,
And once never trusted anyone
Over thirty.

TRUE LOVE

It's true love because
I put on eyeliner and a concerto and make pungent
    observations about the great issues of the day
Even when there's no one here but him,
And because
I do not resent watching the Green Bay Packers
Even though I am philosophically opposed to football,
And because
When he is late for dinner and I know he must be either
    having an affair or lying dead in the middle of the street,
I always hope he's dead.

It's true love because
If he said quit drinking martinis but I kept drinking them
    and the next morning I couldn't get out of bed,
He wouldn't tell me he told me,
And because
He is willing to wear unironed undershorts
Out of respect for the fact that I am philosophically opposed
    to ironing,
And because
If his mother was drowning and I was drowning and he had
    to choose one of us to save,
He says he'd save me.

It's true love because
When he went to San Francisco on business while I had to
    stay home with the painters and the exterminator and the
    baby who was getting the chicken pox,
He understood why I hated him,
And because
When I said that playing the stock market was juvenile and
    irresponsible and then the stock I wouldn't let him buy
    went up twenty-six points,
I understood why he hated me,
And because
Despite cigarette cough, tooth decay, acid indigestion,
    dandruff, and other features of married life that tend to
    dampen the fires of passion,
We still feel something
We can call
True love.

PEOPLE & OTHER AGGRAVATIONS

PEOPLE & OTHER AGGRAVATIONS

I'm having twelve for dinner and the butcher won't deliver.
I forgot my mother's birthday and she's brooding.
Computers keep on dunning me for bills I paid six months
    ago,
And I'm also including air pollution, Richard Nixon, germ
    warfare, the Pill, people . . . and other aggravations.

Penn Central only answers me with tape-recorded messages.
Our pre-school's split on cookies versus crackers.
The girl my husband hired is about to proposition him,
Not to mention hijackers, the SST, race relations, the Joint
    Chiefs of Staff, people . . . and other aggravations.

My in-laws say my attitude is very uncooperative.
The dentist found my gums in poor condition.
The card I mailed a month ago still hasn't reached East
    Paterson,
And there are, in addition, the urban crisis, William Buckley,
    the sex revolution, inflation, people . . . and other
    aggravations.

The first-grade teacher tells me that my son said dirty things
    to her.
Don't ask what I would give to get a plumber.

The friends who just broke up insist I have to choose whose
    side I'm on,
Plus the long hot summer, overpopulation, John Birchers,
    the bomb, people . . . and other aggravations.

My forty-dollar Dynel braid is stuck with Double-Bubble
    gum.
The car (third time this week) has flunked inspection.
Our broker has advised me of some alternate insurance
    plans,
But none of them provides complete protection against
Cigarettes,
Cholesterol,
Weathermen,
The ABM,
CBS,
NBC,
Drug addiction,
DDT,
People . . . and other aggravations.

A WOMEN'S LIBERATION
MOVEMENT WOMAN

When it's snowing and I put on all the galoshes
While he reads the paper,
Then I want to become a
Women's Liberation Movement woman.
And when it's snowing and he looks for the taxi
While I wait in the lobby,
Then I don't.
And when it's vacation and I'm in charge of mosquito bites
    and poison ivy and car sickness
While he's in charge of swimming,
Then I want to become a
Women's Liberation Movement woman.
And when it's vacation and he carries the trunk and the
    overnight bag and the extra blankets
While I carry the wig case,
Then I don't.
And when it's three in the morning and the baby definitely
    needs a glass of water and I have to get up and bring it
While he keeps my place warm,
Then I want to become a
Women's Liberation Movement woman.

And when it's three in the morning and there is definitely a
    murderer-rapist in the vestibule and he has to get up and
    catch him
While I keep his place warm,
Then I don't.

And after dinner, when he talks to the company
While I clean the broiler
(because I am a victim of capitalism, imperialism, male
    chauvinism, and also Playboy magazine),
And afternoons, when he invents the telephone and wins the
    Dreyfus case and writes War and Peace
While I sort the socks
(because I am economically oppressed, physically exploited,
    psychologically mutilated, and also very insulted),
And after he tells me that it is genetically determined that
    the man makes martinis and the lady makes the beds
(because he sees me as a sex object, an earth mother, a
    domestic servant, and also dumber than he is),
Then I want to become a
Women's Liberation Movement woman.

And after I contemplate
No marriage, no family, no shaving under my arms,
And no one to step on a cockroach whenever I need him,
Then I don't.

THE GOURMET

My husband grew up eating lox in New Jersey,
But now he eats saumon fumé.
The noshes he once used to nosh before dinner
He's calling hors d'oeuvres variés.
And food is cuisine since he learned how to be a gourmet.

He now has a palate instead of a stomach
And must have his salad après,
His ris de veau firm, and his port salut runny,
All ordered, of course, en français,
So the waiter should know he is serving a full-fledged
    gourmet.

No meal is complete without something en croute, a-
Mandine, béchamel, en gelée,
And those wines he selects with the care that a surgeon
Transplanting a heart might display.
He keeps sniffing the corks since he learned how to be a
    gourmet.

The tans some folks get from a trip to St. Thomas
He gets from the cerises flambés,
After which he requires, instead of a seltzer,
A cognac or Grand Marnier,

With a toast to the chef from my husband the nouveau
    gourmet.

The words people use for a Chartres or a Mozart
He's using to praise a soufflé.
He reads me aloud from James Beard and Craig Claiborne
The way others read from Corneille.
And he's moved by a mousse since he learned how to be a
    gourmet.

But back in New Jersey, whenever we visit,
They don't know from pouilly-fuissé.
They're still serving milk in the glass from the jelly.
They still cook the brisket all day.
And a son who can't finish three helpings is not a gourmet.

LESSONS

She was taught
If you don't get married you'll wind up a very lonely person
    staring at the four walls, and
He was taught
If you don't finish law school you'll wind up an object of pity
    and contempt selling ties in an East Orange
    haberdashery, and
She was taught
If you don't put a little something aside every week you'll
    wind up a very lonely person being thrown out on the
    sidewalk, and
He was taught
If you lend a friend your sport jacket he'll perspire under the
    arms and it won't come out at the cleaners and you'll wind
    up resentful, and
She was taught
If you don't have Blue Cross and Blue Shield you'll wind up a
    very lonely person delirious in a hospital ward, and
He was taught
If you go to bed with girls they'll lie and say they're pregnant
    and you'll wind up having to marry them, but
She changed her name to Maya, and
He changed his name to Orféo, and
They're living in a commune in the country

With collective housekeeping and organically grown
   vegetables and the kinds of shatteringly honest
   relationships
That are only possible between men and women
Who have renounced flush toilets and the telephone
   company, and
As a result of working in the fields, and
Washing in the streams, and
Wearing simple homespun robes they
Have freed their senses from the tyranny of the intellect, and
Tuned in to the music of the cosmos, and
Plumbed the secret depths of their innermost beings, but
She's still putting a little something aside every week, and
He's still not lending his jacket . . .
Just in case.

A BEAUTIFUL PERSON

Her exercise classes are putting new tone in her muscles.
Her skin doctor's scraping off all the old skin from her face.
Her colorist just changed her hair from champagne to peach
melba.
And as soon as her glands are replaced at the clinic in
Zurich,
Audrey my girlfriend is going to be
A Beautiful Person.

She's buying the co-op that Charlotte Ford once almost lived
in.
She's buying the dresses that Women's Wear says Jackie
wears.
She's buying a dog who's a niece of the Duchess of
Windsor's,
And as soon as she's had an affair with Mike Nichols' third
cousin,
Audrey my girlfriend is going to be
A Beautiful Person.

A very now rock group is playing at all of her parties.
A very now underground filmmaker's filming her thumbs.
A very now artist is doing her portrait in latex.
And as soon as Cesar Chavez comes to stay for the week end,

Audrey my girlfriend is going to be
A Beautiful Person.

She's learning the right things to want at the Parke-Bernet
     gallery.
She's learning the right way to eat and pronounce a coquille.
She's learning what charity balls have the chicest diseases.
And as soon as she's found someone chic-er than me to make
     friends with,
Audrey my girlfriend is going to be
A Beautiful Person.

REMEMBRANCE OF
CHRISTMAS PAST

They let the children out of school too early.
I left the Christmas shopping till too late.
Each day we had a holiday excursion,
Which gave us the entire week to wait in line for
Movies by Disney,
Gift-wrapping by Lord & Taylor,
And everyone's restrooms.

On Christmas Eve we started to assemble
The easy-to-assemble telescope
And fire truck with forty-seven pieces.
By midnight it was plain there was no hope without
An astronomer,
A mechanical engineer,
And two psychiatrists.

We rose at dawn to three boys singing Rudolph.
We listened numbly to their shouts of glee.
The kitten threw up tinsel on the carpet.
The fire truck collided with the tree, requiring
One rug shampoo,
Several Band-aids,
And Scotch before breakfast.

I bought my husband shirts – wrong size, wrong colors,
And ties he said he couldn't be caught dead in.
I'd hinted Saint Laurent or something furry.
He bought me flannel gowns to go to bed in, also
A Teflon frying pan,
A plaid valise,
And The Weight Watchers Cook Book.

The turkey was still frozen at eleven.
At noon my eldest boy spilled Elmer's glue.
At five I had a swell Excedrin headache,
The kind that lasts till January two . . . but
Merry Christmas
And Happy New Year,
I think.

IDA, THE ONE WHO SUFFERS

Whatever happens to me
Has already happened to Ida, the one who suffers,
Only worse,
And with complications,
And her surgeon said it's a miracle she survived,
And her team of lawyers is suing for half a million,
And her druggist gave a gasp when he read the prescription,
And her husband swore he never saw such courage,
Because (though it may sound like bragging) she's not a
    complainer,
Which is why the nurse was delighted to carry her bedpan,
And her daughter flew home from the sit-in in order to visit,
And absolute strangers were begging to give blood
    donations,
And the man from Prudential even had tears in his eyes,
Because (though it may sound like bragging) everyone loves
    her,
Which is why both her sisters were phoning on day rates
    from Dayton,
And her specialist practically forced her to let him make
    house calls,
And the lady who cleans kept insisting on coming in
    Sundays,

And the cousins have canceled the Cousins Club annual
    meeting,
And she's almost embarrassed to mention how many
    presents
Keep arriving from girlfriends who love her all over the
    country,
All of them eating their hearts out with worry for Ida,
The one who suffers
The way other people
Enjoy.

SANDRA SHAPIRO IS SUCH
A GOOD MOTHER

Sandra Shapiro is such a good mother. She says
That if she exposes her children to Winnie the Pooh and The
   Nutcracker Suite and the Hayden Planetarium,
They'll be accepted at Harvard. And she says
That if she exposes her children to black people and poor
   people and Jewish people who are married to non-Jewish
   people,
They'll vote Democratic. And she says
That if she teaches her children (frankly and openly and
   affirmationally) that having babies is a wonderful
   experience but not yet,
They'll thank her someday for being
Such a good mother.

Sandra Shapiro is such a good mother. She says
That if she takes her children on nice wholesome family
   outings like picnics and bike rides,
They won't smoke pot. And she says
That if she buys her children jigsaw puzzles and coloring
   books instead of machine guns and cowboy guns and
   deathray guns,
They won't invade Indochina. And she says
That if she teaches her children (firmly and fearlessly and

uncompromisingly) to always follow the dictates of their
conscience but not yet,
They'll thank her someday for being
Such a good mother.

Sandra Shapiro is such a good mother. She says
That if she assures her children that they don't have to spend
a single penny of their allowance on her birthday present
unless they truly want to,
They'll truly want to. And she says
That if she assures her children that while she would never
dream of prying she is warmly interested in anything they
might want to tell her,
They'll tell her everything. And she says
That if she teaches her children (humbly and modestly and
self-effacingly) that they'll thank her someday for being
Such a good mother,
Maybe someday they'll thank her,
But not yet.

SWAPPING

I like to keep up with the new aberrations
And here's what I recently read:
The latest in lust is the swapping of spouses.
The old-fashioned marriage, it's said,
Is just for the frigid, repressed, and neurotic,
Which no modern wife wants to be.
But nobody asks can he swap with my husband.

Is something the matter with me?

It's claimed that the switching of partners produces
A soundness of body and mind
And feelings of intimate group satisfaction
That couples can't manage to find
In cook-outs and bridge clubs and zoning board meetings
And fund drives to build the school gym.
But nobody asks will I swap her my husband.

Is something the matter with him?

Abandoned, insatiable, pulsing with hunger,
It all seems a terrible strain.
Now why did they have to go make things so fancy
When I've been enjoying them plain?

Erotica hasn't appeared at our parties.
We're still talking kids and clogged pipes.
And nobody asks can we swap with each other.

I guess we don't look like the types.

LOVE STORY

When Jenny my sitter got married to Herb
They agreed she would keep her own name.
Fidelity wasn't important, they said.
And he'd do the dusting while she earned the bread.
And they certainly wouldn't have babies. Instead,
They'd adopt.

She promised to master the tire and jack.
He promised to weep without shame.
(For males must express their emotions, they said.)
And she'd get a Master's while he baked the bread.
And they wouldn't be shocked to find three in their bed.
They'd adapt.

He married in bells, army surplus, and beard.
She married sans bra and sans shoes.
They gave all their presents to poor folks in Ghent.
And she swore if next season their union was rent
That she'd starve before even so much as a cent
She'd accept.

They left on their Yamaha happily stoned.
We're waiting to hear the bad news.
Assured, of course, it will never work out

Since they haven't a clue what real life is about
And besides, if they make it, we'll all start to doubt
Everything.

DECAY

There are laugh lines on my face but I'm not laughing.
I start yawning if I'm out much after twelve.
The latest dances give me lower back pain
And what's sitting on the shelves of my medicine chest I
    won't even discuss.

Excessive garlic irritates my colon.
Excessive coffee irritates my nerves.
Eight specialists are working on my problems
And it suddenly occurs to me that they now call my beauty
    marks moles.

The parts of me that proudly pointed upward
Are slowly taking on a downward droop.
I'm puffing when I reach the second landing
And I know Group Health rates better than I know
    everything I wanted to know about sex.

My shoulder's getting stiffer with each season.
The small print's getting blurrier each week.
The systems which I counted on forever
Are surrendering to creaks, leaks, blockages, and never
    mind what else.

The woman in my head is young and perfect.
The real one has to buy supportive hose.
So I'm waiting for serenity and wisdom,
Which, I'm assured, are supposed to make me feel much
better about this whole thing.

THE FIRST FULL-FLEDGED
FAMILY REUNION

The first full-fledged family reunion
Was held at the seashore
With 9 pounds of sturgeon
7 pounds of corned beef
1 nephew who got the highest mark on an intelligence test
   ever recorded in Hillside, New Jersey
4 aunts in pain taking pills
1 cousin in analysis taking notes
1 sister-in-law who makes a cherry cheese cake a person
   would be happy to pay to eat
5 uncles to whom what happened in the stock market
   shouldn't happen to their worst enemy
1 niece who is running away from home the minute the
   orthodontist removes her braces
1 cousin you wouldn't believe it to look at him only likes
   fellows
1 nephew involved with a person of a different racial
   persuasion which his parents are taking very well
1 brother-in-law with a house so big you could get lost and
   carpeting so thick you could suffocate and a mortgage so
   high you could go bankrupt
1 uncle whose wife is a saint to put up with him

1 cousin who has made such a name for himself he was
  almost Barbra Streisand's obstetrician
1 cousin who has made such a name for himself he was
  almost Jacob Javits' CPA
1 cousin don't ask what he does for a living
1 niece it wouldn't surprise anyone if next year she's playing
  at Carnegie Hall
1 nephew it wouldn't surprise anyone if next year he's
  sentenced to Leavenworth
2 aunts who go to the same butcher as Philip Roth's mother
And me wanting approval from all of them.

A LOT TO GIVE EACH OTHER

He was born before television, and
She was born after running boards, and
He was born before Saran Wrap, and
She was born after the cha cha, and
Although he isn't quite sure which one is Ringo and which
    one is Paul, and
She isn't quite sure which ones are the Andrews Sisters and
    which ones are the Mills Brothers,
They feel they've got a lot to give each other.

He worries about his prostate, and
She worries about her acne, and
He worries about good investments, and
She worries about bad vibrations, and
Although he isn't quite sure which one is Tom Hayden and
    which one is Peter Fonda, and
She isn't quite sure which one is Adolf Hitler and which one
    is Don Ameche,
They feel they've got a lot to give each other.

He doesn't relate to astrology, and
She doesn't relate to deodorants, and
He doesn't relate to acid, and
She doesn't relate to Gelusil, and

Although he isn't quite sure which one is Woodstock and
    which one is Hesse, and
She isn't quite sure which one is Pearl Harbor and which one
    is Veronica Lake,
They feel they've got a lot to give each other.

She wants the baby after they're married, and
He wants the baby before they're married, and
She wants a high-rise with an answering service and
    doormen, and
He wants a crash pad with mattresses and Weathermen, and
Although they aren't quite sure which one adjusted and
    which one sold out,
They feel they've got a lot to give each other.

ANTI-HEROINE

I'd planned to be Heathcliff's Cathy, Lady Brett,
Nicole or Dominique or Scarlett O'Hara.
I hadn't planned to be folding up the laundry
In uncombed hair and last night's smudged mascara,
An expert on buying Fritos, cleaning the cat box,
Finding lost sneakers, playing hide-and-seek,
And other things unknown to Heathcliff's Cathy,
Scarlett, Lady Brett, and Dominique.

Why am I never running through the heather?
Why am I never raped by Howard Roark?
Why am I never going to Pamplona
Instead of Philadelphia and Newark?
How did I ever wind up with an Irving
When what I'd always had in mind was Rhett,
Or someone more appropriate to Cathy,
Dominique, Nicole, or Lady Brett.

I saw myself as heedless, heartless, headstrong,
An untamed woman searching for her mate.
And there he is – with charcoal, fork, and apron,
Prepared to broil some hot dogs on the grate.
I haven't wrecked his life or his digestion
With unrequited love or jealous wrath. He

Doesn't know that secretly I'm Scarlett,
Dominique, Nicole, or Brett, or Cathy.

Why am I never cracking up in Zurich?
Why am I never languishing on moors?
Why am I never spoiled by faithful mammys
Instead of spraying ant spray on the floors?
The tricycles are cluttering my foyer.
The Pop Tart crumbs are sprinkled on my soul.
And every year it's harder to be Cathy,
Dominique, Brett, Scarlett, and Nicole.

THE WORLD TRAVELER

I wish I were one of those spunky women
Who dash off to Africa
With a cleverly packed overnight bag and a pith helmet
Without always thinking
Is there a dentist,
And can I buy Kleenex,
And where will I find the name
Of a good dry cleaners.

I wish I were one of those spunky women
Who climb the Matterhorn,
And race Maseratis,
And run barefoot through the Bois de Boulogne,
Without always thinking
That I'll step on a rusty nail
And need a tetanus shot.

I wish I were one of those spunky women
Who travel around the world on freighters,
And fight in doomed revolutions,
And sleep with some dark stranger in Algiers,
Without always thinking
That the stranger will talk about me
In New Jersey.

I wish I were one of those spunky women . . .
But as I sit here on this plane from Dulles to London,
With twenty pounds of overweight in aspirin,
A heating pad and Tums and Kaopectate,
And throat spray and an extra pair of glasses
(Suppose the first pair breaks in a pub in Chelsea?),
Wondering whether the sitter's rejecting my children
And whether I'll go down in flames reading Time magazine,
Then it all seems a high price to pay
Just to be
Spunky.

DOWN AND OUT IN LONDON

In London I didn't see the Beatles.
In London I didn't see the Stones.
In London I didn't see Peter Sellers telling mod kinky stories
    to Princess Margaret and Anthony Armstrong-Jones
While internationally famous hairdressers
And internationally skinny models
Did corrupt but trendy things to each other
At private clubs.

In London I saw Museums and Towers.
In London I saw them change the guard.
In London I ate a lot of meat pies with one piece of meat
    blended with three pounds of lard,
Followed by a walk in the rain
And another one of those afternoon teas
With the shredded lettuce leaves
On tissue paper.

In London I'd planned to change my image.
In London I haven't changed a thing.
In London I'm standing on the King's Road
With wet feet,
Indigestion,
The wrong hemline,

A run in my pantyhose,
The Oxford Book of English Verse,
And a continuing inability to swing
Even in London.

OUT ON THE ALPS

As daylight breaks over the Alps (Courchevel 1850),
And the right thing to do is roll over and sleep until ten,
My husband is nudging my black-and-blue thigh with his
    kneecap,
And saying (hey, great!) that it's time to go skiing again.
So I put on the stretch pants that quit stretching over my
    stomach
When I learned how to eat seven courses at lunch and dîner,
Then I put on the sweaters, the parka, the hood, and the ski
    boots
(They're hell in the morning but tend to get worse through
    the day),
And I leave the warm room with its blankets and Agatha
    Christies
To go where it's snowy and windy and cold and not safe,
Ignoring the pain in my shoulders, arms, thighs, calves, and
    ankles,
Plus the place where the heel in my boot is beginning to
    chafe.
And we're off in the télécabine to the top of the mountain
And I'm hoping the motor won't stop as we sway over peaks,
And the cable won't snap as we hang forty feet from abysses,
And that terrible sound is the wind and not somebody's
    shrieks.

Now (isn't it lovely!) we're here with the treetops below us.
And my skis aren't on but already I've fallen down twice
Just from taking a look at the trail – narrow, vertical, fatal.
(And here comes my husband, Jean-Claude, with some
    words of advice.)
Well, I've just cut my thumb in the process of closing my
    bindings,
And my goggles are fogged and my nerves inexpressibly
    shot.
But I'm off with a wild snowplow turn and a large crowd of
    Frenchmen
Who keep schussing past me with shouts of à gauche and à
    droite.
And I know I could tell which was which if I wasn't
    attempting
To bend at the knees, shift my weight, not go over that ledge,
Which explains why I've skied off the trail and am presently
    standing
In uncharted mountains and up to my fesses in the neige,
Where I'm dreaming of tropical isles, riding surf in bikinis,
But willing to settle for home, pushing kids in the carriage,
And firmly convinced that the Alps may be swell for the
    Killys,
But not for a person who's only a skier by marriage.

DAVID IS DYING TO GET MARRIED

David is dying to get married.
He is dying to share
His heart, his insights, and the unspoiled island in the
    Caribbean where he is the only American who goes there
With someone feminine enough and intelligent enough and
    mature enough to understand
That when he's hostile it's because he's feeling threatened,
And when he's vicious it's because he feels unloved,
And when he's paranoid, sadistic, depressed, or sexually
    inadequate,
It's simply because
She has failed him. Yes,
David is dying to get married.
He is dying to share
His fishtank, his discounts, and the unspoiled restaurant in
    Chinatown where he is the only Caucasian who eats there
With someone secure enough and subtle enough and
    grateful enough to understand
That when he's rigid it's because he has high standards,
And when he's violent it's because he has no choice,
And when he's manic, suicidal, or having trouble sleeping,
It's simply because
She has failed him. Yes,
David is dying to get married.

To a woman like Lauren Bacall but a bit more submissive.
To a woman like Melina Mercouri but a bit more refined.
To a woman who understands that in order to share
His loves, his hates, his hopes, his fears, his low license plate,
  his high tax bracket, and his rent-controlled apartment
  with the terrace where he and his mother are the only
  people who live there,
She'd better not fail him.

STARTING ON MONDAY

Starting on Monday I'm living on carrots and bouillon.
Starting on Monday I'm bidding the bagel adieu.
I'm switching from Hersheys with almonds to gaunt and
    anaemic,
And people will ask me could that skinny person be you.
I'll count every calorie from squash (half a cup, 47)
To Life Saver (8), stalk of celery (5), pepper ring (2),
Starting on Monday.

Starting on Monday I'll jog for a mile in the morning.
(That's after the sit-ups and push-ups and touching my
    toes.)
The gratification I once used to seek in lasagna
I'll find on the day that I have to go buy smaller clothes.
I'll turn my attention from infantile pleasures like Clark Bars
To things like the song of a bird and the scent of a rose,
Starting on Monday.

Starting on Monday my will will be stronger than brownies,
And anything more than an unsalted egg will seem crude.
My inner-thigh fat and my upper-arm flab will diminish.
My cheeks will be hollowed, my ribs will begin to protrude.
The bones of my pelvis will make their initial appearance –

A testament to my relentless abstention from food,
Starting on Monday.

But Tuesday a friend came for coffee and brought
    homemade muffins.
And Wednesday I had to quit jogging because of my back.
On Thursday I read in the paper an excess of egg yolk
Would clog up my vessels and certainly cause an attack.
On Friday we ate at the Goldfarbs. She always makes cream
    sauce,
And always gets sulky if people don't eat what she makes.
On Saturday evening we went with the kids to a drive-in.
I begged for a Fresca but all they were selling were shakes.
On Sunday my stomach oozed over the top of my waistband,
And filled with self-loathing I sought consolation in pie
And the thought that Onassis could bribe me with yachts and
    with emeralds
But still I'd refuse to taste even a single French fry . . .
Starting on Monday.

ALAN THE DROP-OUT

My cousin Alan the drop-out
Is giving the family such heartache
That already he's caused one angina,
A skin rash, and plenty of migraines,
And it's clear that he's killing his mother,
According to mine.

My cousin Alan the drop-out,
With brains like an Einstein or Goldberg
And a guaranteed future in Orlon,
Is living in worse than a cellar
With a girlfriend a mother could die from,
According to mine.

My cousin Alan the drop-out,
Who dressed like a playboy from Florida
And everyone swore was Rock Hudson,
Now looks like King Kong with a headband,
And a mother could faint just to see him,
According to mine.

My cousin Alan the drop-out,
A person who once wouldn't jaywalk,
Keeps going to jail like a Scarface

For doing fresh things to the System,
And the shame gives his mother hot flashes,
According to mine.

My cousin Alan the drop-out,
Is writing his memoirs for Harper's
And people in suits want his viewpoint
On stations both local and network.
He's posing for pictures at Newsweek
And auditions tomorrow for Susskind,
And his mother could learn to enjoy it,
According to mine.

THE LADY NEXT DOOR

The lady next door,
Who weighs eight pounds less than I do
And wears peach face gleamer and tawny lip gloss to take out
    the garbage,
Has lately been looking at my husband
As if he were someone like Robert Redford,
And she were someone like Ali MacGraw,
And I were someone like Mother of the Year.

The lady next door,
Whose children go to analysts and Choate,
And whose favorite drink is a dry white burgundy with a
    smidgen of crème de cassis,
Has lately been looking at my husband
As if he were someone with inexpressible yearnings,
And she were someone who majored in how to express them,
And I were someone who played a lot of hockey.

The lady next door,
Has lately been looking at my husband,
Who has lately been looking back,
Leaving me to contemplate
Murder,
Suicide,

Adult education courses,
An affair with one of those rich Greek eighty-year-olds who
    prefer younger women,
An affair with one of those alienated twenty-year-olds who
    prefer older women,
Or maybe an affair
With the man next door,
Who has Cardin suits, a rapier wit, a Ferrari,
As well as close friends in the arts,
And who has lately been looking at me
As if I were someone who knew how to sew on buttons,
And he were someone who needed someone to sew them,
And my husband were only someone who deserved
The lady next door.

POLITICALLY PERFECT

Sally and Stu
Were married by a militant minister
(He was bitten by a Birmingham police dog),
Moved to an integrated neighborhood
(Thirty-four per cent were Black or Other),
Turned down a low-cost trip to Greece
(For obvious reasons),
And have always strived to be
Politically perfect
By displaying aggressive bumper stickers,
Boycotting non-returnable bottles,
And including, at every cocktail party,
One American Indian, one Draft Resister, and Ralph Nader.

Sally and Stu
Were admitted to the nicest New Left circles
(Published writers, sometimes even Mailer),
Solicited for all the finest causes
(Panthers, Moratoriums, Defense Funds),
Advocated the dismantling of the war machine and the
    smashing of the major corporations and the total
    restructuring of society
(Without, of course, condoning undue violence),
And have always strived to be

Politically perfect
By giving generously,
Picketing profusely,
And including, at every Christmas party,
One unwed mother, one well-intentioned bomber, and the
    maid.

They have always strived to be
Politically perfect – but

Recently they met a sweet policeman
And a rotten revolutionary,
And started feeling hostile to all muggers
Regardless of color or creed,
And then he discovered that he couldn't say 'pig' or 'right
    on'
Without sounding insincere,
And then she discovered that she couldn't say 'male sexist
    oppressor'
Without sounding insincere,
And when he asked her
Was she capable of taking off her clothes and painting an
    anti-war symbol on her stomach and floating across the
    Potomac in the interests of world peace
And her answer was no,
And when she asked him
Was he capable of annihilating his racist parents and his
    racist brother Arnold and that racist little blonde he used
    to go with in the interests of world brotherhood,

And his answer was no,
They knew
They'd never be
Politically perfect.

THE WRITERS

I write in the bedroom with unsorted laundry,
A crib, and a baby who hollers.
My husband the writer gets gold velvet chairs,
A couch that cost four hundred dollars,
A wall-to-wall carpet, bright red and all wool,
And a desk big enough to play pool on.
I type in quadruplicate, two sets for me
And two for the baby to drool on,
In a setting conducive to grocery lists
And decisions like chopped steak or flounder.
Did Emily Dickinson have to write poems
With diaper-rash ointment around her?
Did Elizabeth Browning stop counting the ways
When Robert said one hot pastrami?
Excuse me, the big boys just came home from school
And they're yelling their heads off for mommy.

My husband the writer makes long-distance calls
To people too famous to mention.
The closest I get to the great outside world
Is listening on the extension
Or reading old Digests while taking the kids
For their flu shots and antibiotics.
(Everyone knows that the mother who works

Will doubtlessly bring up psychotics
Unless she's right there when the chicken pox pop
Or they're stricken with gnat bites and toe aches.)
Did Edna St. Vincent Millay rise at dawn
For a first-grade production called Snowflakes?
Did Marianne Moore put her symbols aside
To wipe Quaker Oats off the table?
Excuse me, my husband would like a cold beer.
I'll be back just as soon as I'm able.

The baby is sleeping, the beds have been made,
And I've mopped where the kitchen was muddy.
My husband the writer has finished the Times
And he's vanishing into his study,
Where no one would dare to disturb his deep thoughts
(Or the half-hour nap he requires).
I've gone to the cleaners and picked up dessert
And I even put air in the tires
Before sitting down at my second-hand Royal.
(He just bought a new Olivetti.)
Did Miss Amy Lowell find Patterns besmirched
With dribbles of Junior Spaghetti?
Does Phyllis McGinley refrain from her rhymes
Whenever her garden needs spraying?
Excuse me, the dishwasher's gone on the blink.
Maybe I'll switch to crocheting.

WHEN I GROW UP

When I grow up I'll stop believing
That if Paul Newman really got to know me he'd divorce
    Joanne Woodward,
And I'll stop believing
That it wouldn't be so impossible for a teenage boy to
    mistake me for a teenage girl,
And I'll stop believing
That someday I'll find a beauty cream which, after I massage
    it gently into my skin every night for three weeks before
    retiring,
You'll never recognize me.
When I grow up I'll stop believing
That people who own paintings of blobs and stripes have a
    better grasp of the universe than people who own
    paintings of sunsets,
And I'll stop believing
That people who buy VWs and Volvos are intrinsically more
    humane than people who buy Lincoln Continentals,
And I'll stop believing
That people who admire people like Dick Cavett have nobler
    aspirations
Than people who admire Johnny Carson.
When I grow up I'll stop believing
That the Mafia is run by distinguished-looking gentlemen

with graying temples and wonderful home lives,
And I'll stop believing
That the Republican party is run by insincere-looking
     gentlemen with short socks and terrible sex lives,
And I'll stop believing
That an Episcopalian is anyone who knew about sailboats,
     napkin rings, Hepplewhite, and self-assurance
Twenty years before I did.
When I grow up I'll stop believing
That I'm destined to become the toast of Broadway,
And I'll stop believing
That I'm destined to become the Dean of Smith,
And I'll stop believing
That I'm destined to become a love goddess, a tennis
     champion, Madame Curie, or Golda Meir
When I grow up.

Persephone Books publishes forgotten fiction and
non-fiction by unjustly neglected authors. The following
titles are available:

If you have enjoyed this Persephone book why not telephone or write to us for a free copy of the Persephone Catalogue and the current Persephone Quarterly? All Persephone books ordered from us cost £10 or three for £27 plus £2 postage per book.

PERSEPHONE BOOKS LTD
59 Lamb's Conduit Street
London WC1N 3NB

Telephone: 020 7242 9292
Fax: 020 7242 9272
sales@persephonebooks.co.uk
www.persephonebooks.co.uk

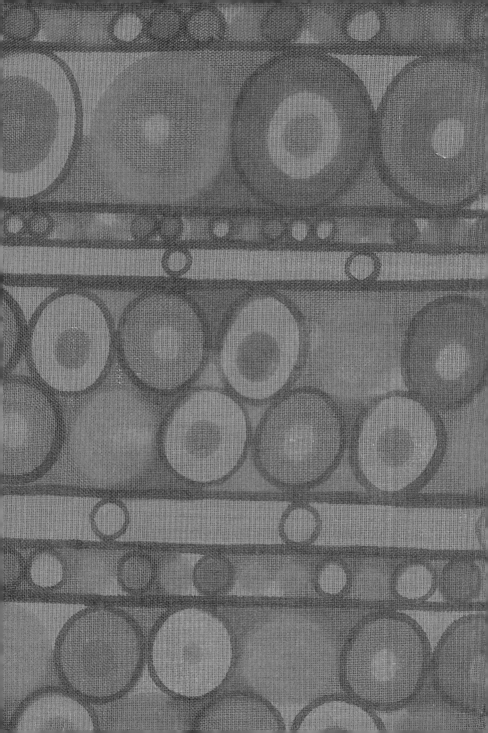